KINGFISHER
VOYAGES

WILD
WEATHER

CAROLINE HARRIS

QUOTATIONS AND FOREWORD BY
WARREN FAIDLEY

KINGFISHER

BOSTON

WELCOME TO THE VOYAGE

Storm chaser
Warren Faidley has been chasing storms for more than 20 years. He is a photographer who takes amazing pictures of extreme weather and has become an expert on storm behavior.

Dear Voyager,
My name is Warren Faidley, and I will be your storm chaser guide as you journey through this book. In the next few pages we will look at what shapes Earth's weather. Then, in Chapter One, we will experience the full force of water, from incredible clouds to devastating floods. In Chapter Two we will track awe-inspiring storms, including hurricanes and tornadoes. Finally, we will travel through extremes of heat and cold. As you explore the book, you will find extra features to help you on your way. You can turn the transparent pages to see an amazing lightning show or the path of a twister or unfold the dramatic story of a drought. And you can read my quotations to learn about my own experiences with wild weather.

The power of the elements
From floods to wildfires and from dust storms to avalanches, wild weather takes many different forms. Extreme weather can also cause terrible damage and loss of lives.

On the trail
Storm chasing can be dangerous, especially if you do not know what you are doing. Warren is very careful about safety. His storm-chasing truck even has extra-tough glass to protect it from hail.

A storm chaser is someone who tracks down wild weather in order to study, photograph, or simply experience it. Some chasers are scientists who want to learn about what happens inside a storm. Others help predict or spot where a tornado is forming so that the people who live nearby can be warned in advance. The United States has a lot of the world's wildest weather. With my storm-chasing truck, maps, and forecasting equipment, I travel to different parts of the country to capture these events on my camera. In the spring I go on the trail of tornadoes in the Great Plains, and later I catch thunderstorms in the desert around where I live, in Tucson, Arizona. In the late summer and fall hurricanes sometimes hit the south and east coasts.

Warren Faidley

Lighting up the sky
This shot of lightning hitting some storage tanks made Warren famous and meant that he could be a full-time storm chaser. To take the picture, he had to crawl past a nest of black widow spiders.

STORM CHASER'S CALENDAR

October

September

HURRICANES

August

July

THUNDERSTORMS

June

May

April

TORNADOES

THE WEATHER MACHINE

From the lightest shower to the wildest hurricane, our weather is created by three elements—heat from the Sun, water, and air. The way they work together can be thought of as a type of "weather machine." The Sun provides the warmth and light that make life on Earth possible, and its energy powers the weather machine. When sunshine heats the oceans, the seawater evaporates, turning it into its gas form—water vapor—and becoming an invisible part of the air. And as the Sun warms the land and sea, this makes the air just above them become hotter too. As a result, the air rises upward, cooling down as it moves higher. This produces clouds, which in turn lead to storms.

HOT AND COLD

Hottest location
136°F (57.8°C)
Al'Aziziyah, Libya
September 13, 1922

Hottest annual average
94°F (34.4°C)
Dallol, Ethiopia
1960–1966

Greatest 24-hour change
100°F (44°F to −56°F)
Browning, Montana
January 23–24, 1916

Coldest location
-128.6°F (−89.2°C)
Vostok station, Antarctica
July 21, 1983

Earth's path around the Sun

Earth is tilted

Sun

The heating effect of the Sun is the strongest in the tropics, the belt north and south of the equator. Earth has a slight tilt, so different parts of the planet are warmed more at different times of the year, causing the seasons.

Extremes of temperature
The Libyan Desert is one of the hottest places on Earth. In the tropics the Sun is almost overhead throughout the year, which is why the heat is so intense there. Earth's coldest regions are toward the North and South poles. Tall mountain ranges are also icy because the temperature is lower high up in the atmosphere.

Earth is surrounded by a layered blanket of air called the atmosphere. Most of our weather happens in the lowest part, which reaches up around as high as Mount Everest in Asia, but some storms are so powerful that they break through into the next level. Air is almost always moving from one place to another, and this is what we call wind. Some winds blow for immense distances across Earth, while others may be confined to a single river valley. They occur because the Sun heats different parts of the planet's surface by different amounts, creating areas of warmer and cooler air. The winds power the weather machine. They push the clouds, bringing rain, and when blocks of warm and cold air meet, this produces weather systems that can generate dust storms and tornadoes.

Clear blue skies
The air is always pushing on us, even though we are not aware of it. This is called air pressure. When air sinks, it creates an area of high pressure, which often brings clear skies with few clouds, as seen here in New Mexico.

Gray and cloudy skies
Low pressure is often associated with sheets of clouds, as seen here in New Jersey. When the wind blows, it is because air is moving from an area of higher pressure to an area of lower pressure—the air is trying to even itself out.

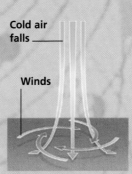

Cold air falls

Winds

In an area of high pressure cold air sinks downward. Winds move out from the bottom.

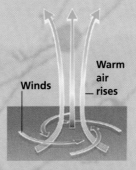

Winds

Warm air rises

In an area of low pressure warm air rises up, creating clouds and rain. Winds move inward near ground level.

BEAUFORT SCALE (wind speed)	
FORCE	**EFFECT**
0 (below 1 mph)	**Calm** Air feels still; smoke rises straight up
1 (1 mph–3 mph)	**Light air** Flags do not move; rising smoke drifts
2 (3.7 mph–6.8 mph)	**Light breeze** Leaves rustle; smoke drifts in direction of wind
3 (7.4 mph–11.8 mph)	**Gentle breeze** Leaves and twigs move; small flags flutter
4 (12.4 mph–18 mph)	**Moderate breeze** Small branches move; paper blows around
5 (18.6 mph–23.6 mph)	**Fresh breeze** Small trees sway; waves with crests form on lakes
6 (24.1 mph–31.6 mph)	**Strong breeze** Large branches sway; hard to use an umbrella
7 (31.6 mph–37.8 mph)	**Near gale** Whole trees sway; hard to walk against wind
8 (38.4 mph–45.9 mph)	**Gale** Twigs snap off trees; wind makes it difficult to walk
9 (46.5 mph–53.3 mph)	**Strong gale** Branches break; tiles and chimneys torn off roofs
10 (53.9 mph–62.6 mph)	**Severe gale** Trees snapped or uprooted by wind
11 (63.2 mph–74.4 mph)	**Violent storm** Trees blown around; cars overturned
12 (more than 74.4 mph)	**Hurricane** Many trees torn up; buildings destroyed

Water covers almost three fourths of Earth's surface. It is the fuel of the weather machine and has an unusual and special quality. It can be found on this planet in its three forms—as solid ice, liquid water, and water vapor gas—all at the same time. The amount of water on the planet always stays around the same, but it shifts between these three forms and moves to different places. In a process called the water cycle water moves from the oceans to the air, where it exists as vapor and then as clouds, before falling as rain, snow, or hail. Eventually, it rejoins the seas, and the cycle begins again. Water's ability to change its form gives our climate its incredible variety. From spectacular flashes of lightning to the roaring descent of an avalanche, it also fuels the types of wild weather that you will read about and explore in the rest of this book.

How rain is born
These tea pickers shelter from heavy rains in Darjeeling, India. As air rises and cools, it can hold less and less water vapor. Clouds form when the vapor becomes tiny droplets of liquid water or, if the cloud is very high up, ice crystals. As droplets knock into each other, they merge to form larger drops. These become too heavy to stay in the air and fall as rain. A raindrop is around 100 times the size of a cloud droplet.

WET AND DRY

Greatest 24-hour rainfall
75 in. (1,870mm)
Cilaos,
Réunion, Indian Ocean
March 15–16, 1952

Greatest annual rainfall
1,058 in. (26,461mm)
Cherrapunji,
Meghalaya, India
August 1860 to July 1861

Wettest location
475 in. (11,872mm) average rainfall per year
Mawsynram,
Meghalaya, India

Driest location
0.02 in. (0.5mm) rainfall per year
Quillagua, Atacama Desert, Chile 1964–2001

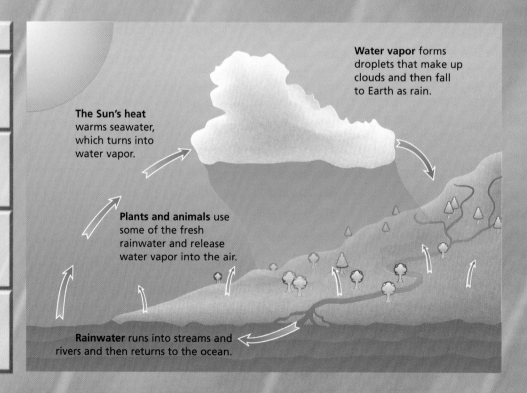

Water vapor forms droplets that make up clouds and then fall to Earth as rain.

The Sun's heat warms seawater, which turns into water vapor.

Plants and animals use some of the fresh rainwater and release water vapor into the air.

Rainwater runs into streams and rivers and then returns to the ocean.

WATER

EXTREME CLOUDS

The wildest storm begins its life as a tiny, unremarkable cloud. If the conditions are right, a small cumulus cloud that is born on a summer morning will grow and grow throughout the heat of the day. It will reach upward until it becomes a menacing tower that stretches from low in the sky to 6 mi. (10km) above the ground—around the height that most aircraft can fly. In the late afternoon or early evening this fully grown, mature storm cloud may release streaks of lightning and balls of hail. As it rains, the cloud usually will lose its energy, break up, and disappear. But sometimes a storm cloud will continue shooting up through the atmosphere, bringing even more extreme weather, including tornadoes.

Flying saucers
When strong winds are forced up over a mountain range, they can cause smooth disks of clouds, like these in Washington state, to appear over the peaks. Called lenticular clouds, they look like a stack of plates—or a UFO (unidentified flying object).

Thunder ahead
A towering cloud, such as this cumulonimbus incus in Colorado, is the type that produces thunderstorms. It has a distinctive shape with a spreading top. This part of the cloud is called the anvil, or thunderhead. It forms when the cloud meets an invisible ceiling of warmer air.

Warning clouds
A domed cloud formation, called mammatus, looms over a church in Alberta, Canada. Mammatus hangs from beneath the anvil of a mature thundercloud and is a sign of severe weather, especially tornadoes.

" I've seen storm clouds suddenly grow *to more than 49,000 feet,* topped with a spectacular circular anvil. *Any small cloud that tries to challenge these giants is sucked in and consumed for fuel. The shapes are amazing.* They look so solid—you can imagine walking up the side *of them.* "

CLOUD FILE

Above 5,000m (16,400 ft.)	**Cirrus** — **Wispy curls** of cirrus are the highest type of cloud.
Above 5,000m (16,400 ft.)	**Cirrocumulus** — **Tufted white** sheets like this are made out of ice crystals.
900m–9,000m (3,000 ft.–29,500 ft.)	**Cumulonimbus** — **Tall nimbus** clouds will bring rain showers.
600m–1,950m (2,000 ft.–6,400 ft.)	**Stratocumulus** — **Lumpy layers** of this cloud are common worldwide.
600m–1,200m (2,000 ft.–4,000 ft.)	**Cumulus** — **Fluffy puffs** with a flat base are seen in the summer.
0m–1,950m (0 ft.–6,400 ft.)	**Stratus** — **Low sheets** of stratus stretch over hundreds of miles.

THUNDERSTORMS

From the ancient Greeks to the Norse people, who lived in Scandinavia, many civilizations have believed in and made offerings to gods of thunder and lightning. Thunderstorms have always been one of nature's most powerful and awe-inspiring events. A single storm can release enough energy to supply the entire United States with electricity for 20 minutes. A flash of lightning is a huge electrical spark. Inside the upper part of a storm cloud ice crystals form because the air is colder at this height. The crystals and water droplets are blown around violently and knock against each other. This creates electric charges—like rubbing a balloon against your hair. When the difference in charge is big enough, electricity leaps from one area to another, creating the lightning flash. We hear thunder because the lightning rapidly superheats the air, making it explode.

High-rise strike
This photograph of the Eiffel Tower in Paris, France, taken in 1902, was one of the first ever to record lightning in a city. Tall buildings, mountains, and radio and TV towers are often struck. The Empire State Building in New York City is hit around 100 times each year.

Lighting up the clouds
The electrical charges that build up in storm clouds can flow only when they are very large—which is why lightning is so bright. Bolts that jump from one cloud to another—or between parts of the same cloud—are called cloud-to-cloud lightning.

LIGHTNING FILE

Around the world: There are 1,800 storms going on at this moment

Stormiest place: Kampala, in Uganda, has storms on around 242 days per year

Width of a lightning bolt: less than an inch

Length: up to 125 mi. (200km)

Fulgurites: "Fossil lightning," produced when a strike melts the soil that it passes through

Ball lightning

This rare type of lightning can appear after a ground strike. Ball lightning is around the size of a beach ball and may roll along or climb up objects before exploding or fading away. Scientists do not know its exact cause.

" Lightning will seek out its target, attracted to even the smallest piece of metal, like a camera tripod or a zipper. When you feel the hair on your arms stand on end, that's when you know it's getting close. You can sense the electrical energy building up. The antennae on my truck will sizzle and pop too, and the radio starts to crackle. "

Cloud-to-ground lightning

There are 100 lightning strikes per second throughout the world, and around one bolt in four hits the ground. The electricity can travel under the ground, so you may be in danger even if you are far away.

Trails through the sky

In cloud-to-air lightning the charge leaps to the surrounding atmosphere. To tell how close a storm is, count the seconds between the lightning flash and the thunderclap. Each five seconds between "flash" and "bang" equals 1 mi. (1.6km).

LIGHTNING STRIKES

Zigzag flashes of lightning cut across the sky. Trees, clouds, and buildings are lit up for a split second with an eerie brightness. Lightning can be spectacular to watch, but it is also extremely dangerous. Throughout the world around 200 people per year are killed by lightning strikes. A single bolt carries enough electricity to power 150 million lightbulbs and heats the air it travels through to 54,000°F (30,000°C) —five times the temperature of the Sun's surface. There are some great survival stories. A park ranger was hit seven times, and his worst injury was the loss of a toe.

WHAT HAPPENS WHEN LIGHTNING STRIKES

1 **Cats run for cover:** Animals like dogs and horses also become nervous before a storm

2 **Thundercloud:** Inside there are strong currents of wind that blow up and down

3 **Raindrops:** Can be huge, as the winds keep them up in the air until they are very heavy

4 **Chaser truck:** Storm chasers have special equipment to track violent storms

5 **Hail:** During a thunderstorm there are often showers of hailstones, which are balls of ice

6 **Cloud-to-ground lightning:** Attracted to metal and will hit tall buildings and chimneys

7 **Cloud-to-air lightning:** Will sometimes be seen even if the storm is too far away to hear

8 **Cloud-to-cloud lightning:** Can light up the inside of a cloud so that it glows like a giant lamp

9 **Fire hazard:** The heat from lightning can make trees explode and start wildfires

10 **Power cut:** Lightning can cause a surge of electricity that knocks out power supplies

FLOODS

Water is vital for all life on Earth, but it can also bring great destruction. Floods cause almost one half of all deaths from natural disasters around the world. Even in less severe floods, people often have to be rescued from the roofs of their water-filled homes, and farm animals may become stranded. If sewage gets into drinking water supplies, typhoid fever, cholera, and other diseases can spread quickly. Most flooding is the result of heavy rainfall, although it can also be caused by melting snow or by enormous waves, called tsunamis, that are triggered by undersea earthquakes. When large rivers overflow, huge areas may remain flooded for many weeks. In 1993 the Mississippi and Missouri rivers in the United States burst their banks at the same time, submerging almost 16,000 square miles.

A region underwater
Hurricanes and tropical storms often result in broadscale, or widespread, flooding. In 2004 rain from Tropical Storm Jeanne battered the city of Gonaives in Haiti for 30 hours. Floods and mud slides destroyed crops and homes, and many people lost their lives. Three fourths of the city was covered by water, and more than 250,000 people were left homeless.

Washed away
Flooding rivers can destroy homes, roads, and bridges as well as cutting off telephone and electric services. Here, the force of water washes away the soil beneath this house in the Italian Alps, until it collapses into the river below.

A flash flood

In December 1999 Cervinara, in southern Italy, was hit by sudden floods when extreme rainfall made streams overflow in the hills around the town. Flash floods occur when huge amounts of rain fall during a short period of time. Although they usually affect only a small area, they are very dangerous because people do not have time to prepare. Flash floods are more likely to occur where the ground cannot absorb much water—such as in rocky, mountainous regions or in cities, where the soil is covered by cement and roads.

EL NIÑO

In 1997 and 1998 global weather was thrown into chaos. In Indonesia vast forest fires raged after months of a drought, filling the air with smoke so thick that drivers had to use headlights at midday. In Peru there were severe floods, and a lake that was 90 mi. (145km) long appeared in a desert that had been dry for 15 years. The cause was El Niño—a current of warm water that pushes through the Pacific Ocean toward South America every five to seven years. This has a dramatic effect on rainfall and temperatures around the world, from Africa to central Europe and Mongolia to the United States.

Storms in California
The El Niño of 1997–1998 fueled huge waves along the coast of California, tornadoes in Florida, and flooding in several U.S. states. Winter temperatures were also higher.

The 1997 El Niño event is shown on this satellite image. The warm current moves east across the Pacific Ocean.

North America

South America

Cool current

Pacific Ocean

Warm El Niño current

Drought in Australia
This is the dried-up bed of Lake Burrendong. Droughts in Australia and Southeast Asia have been linked to El Niño because it makes the winds in the western Pacific drier than normal.

Floods in Brazil
Most of the city of Eldorado had to be evacuated after the local river burst its banks. In El Niño years the warm, moist air brings unusually heavy rains, often causing flooding in South America.

STORMS

HURRICANE ALERT

As a hurricane approaches, you can hear the wind getting stronger. First comes the sound of garbage being blown down the street and tiles falling off of roofs. Then power lines begin to spark. Windows shatter, and trees collapse to the ground as they are uprooted. The huge booms and crashes are the sounds of buildings being ripped apart. Eventually, the wind is so loud that all you can hear is its whistling and roaring. These are the most powerful storms on Earth. The largest contain hundreds of thunderstorms in circling bands that measure up to 600 mi. (970km) across. Even an average hurricane extends over an area that is twice the size of Ireland. Their devastating winds blow at the speed of an Indianapolis 500 race car, with some gusts reaching almost 190 mph (300km/h).

The view from space
Satellite pictures, such as this one of Hurricane Andrew approaching Louisiana in 1992, allow scientists to track a hurricane as it develops. They look for groups of thunderclouds that are beginning to spin. Then they watch to see if an "eye" forms—the circular opening in the middle of the hurricane.

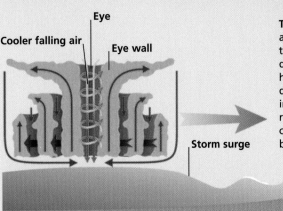

Eye

Cooler falling air

Eye wall

Storm surge

The strongest winds and storms are in the bank of clouds called the eye wall. Warm, moist air is drawn in at the bottom of the hurricane, and cooler air drops down along the eye. Low pressure inside the eye makes the sea level rise, creating a storm surge. This can result in giant waves that batter the coast.

Early warnings
Information from satellites, computers, and radar allows forecasters to warn people where a hurricane is likely to strike. This has helped save many lives.

Evacuation routes
In 1999 a 93-mi. (150-km)-long traffic jam snaked through South Carolina as residents of Charleston fled Hurricane Floyd by driving inland. Before evacuating their homes, people tried to limit hurricane damage by boarding up houses and businesses.

> *" The eye wall was upon us, and I watched as the wind attacked a house. First it got under the heavy storm shutters and started slamming them backward and forward. Seconds later, the windows vanished, and the rest of the house was slowly picked apart. "*

Eyes in the sky
This U.S. Navy aircraft is part of the Airborne Early Warning Squadron, which has tracked hurricanes since the 1940s. Some planes fly directly into the eye, where there are no clouds and the wind is gentle. Flocks of birds are sometimes caught there and are unable to fly out during a storm.

SAFFIR-SIMPSON HURRICANE SCALE (wind speed)

CATEGORY	EFFECT
1 (73 mph– 94 mph)	Slight damage. Trees and shrubs lose leaves and twigs. Storm surge flooding along coastal roads.
2 (95 mph– 109 mph)	Some trees blown over. Damage to mobile homes. Chimneys and tiles blown from roofs. Small boats may break from their moorings.
3 (110 mph– 129 mph)	Leaves stripped off and large trees blown down. Mobile homes destroyed; small buildings damaged. Houses battered by floods.
4 (130 mph– 154 mph)	Extreme damage to windows, roofs, and doors. Mobile homes completely demolished. Floods up to 6 mi. (10km) inland.
5 (more than 154 mph)	Catastrophic damage. Even strongly constructed buildings are affected. Small buildings blown away. Major flood damage.

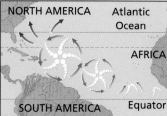

NORTH AMERICA — Atlantic Ocean
AFRICA
SOUTH AMERICA — Equator

Hurricane
Direction of rotation
Path of hurricane

Hurricanes are born in the warm sea off the coast of Africa. Earth's rotation causes a cluster of thunderclouds to spin. This storm then moves northwest across the Atlantic Ocean, becoming stronger as it travels.

HURRICANE LANDFALL

Landfall—when a hurricane crosses onto the shore—is the time that everyone fears most. Towering waves pound the coast, rain pours down, and ferocious winds blast through towns. The violent thunderstorms in the eye wall crackle with lightning, and some hurricanes even produce tornadoes. The result can be floods, mud slides, and the destruction of entire neighborhoods. In 1900 the whole city of Galveston, Texas, was covered by water. In other parts of the world hurricanes go by different names. In the northwest Pacific, which has the most severe storms, they are called typhoons. In the south Pacific and Indian oceans they are known as cyclones. As a hurricane moves over land or cooler seas, it begins to weaken as its "fuel supply" of heat and moisture is cut off. But it still has the power to cause destruction, as the remaining clouds may drop enough rain to cause serious flooding inland.

Atlantic hurricane damage
Atlantic hurricanes usually strike the Caribbean and southern U.S., especially Florida, but sometimes their effects are felt farther away. In 1987 this forest in Kent, England, was flattened when wind from the remains of a hurricane intensified a storm over southern Great Britain.

Hurricane Andrew
Arriving at 5 A.M. on a Sunday morning in August 1992, Andrew is one of only three Category 5 hurricanes to have hit the U.S. since records began. The 16-ft. (5-m) storm surge ripped boats from their moorings, dragging some hundreds of feet inland. In just a few minutes around 15,000 boats were destroyed.

An expensive storm

This house in South Dade County, Florida, is one of more than 125,000 that were wrecked or destroyed by Hurricane Andrew. Around 250,000 people lost their homes. It was the most expensive natural disaster in U.S. history, causing more than $25 billion worth of damage.

Path of destruction

The high winds in the eye wall of
Hurricane Andrew cut a trail 25 mi. (40km)
wide. This Miami, Florida, trailer park was turned into
a field of rubble. But the worst damage from a hurricane is
usually the result of flooding, caused by the storm surge and torrential rains.

TORNADO TOUCHDOWN

Tornadoes are the ultimate in wild weather. When the spiraling funnel of a tornado drops down from a storm cloud to touch the ground, there is a boom that sounds like a huge explosion. The shape has been compared to a giant tail lashing across the landscape. A tornado can rip a house from its foundations, fling it through the air, and leave it in pieces. This extreme type of storm, also known as a twister, is a column of powerful winds that spins at more than 300 mph (500km/h), the speed of the world's fastest train. Tornadoes vary in strength and can last from a few minutes to more than an hour. The most violent twisters are in the United States, where around 1,000 are reported every year, but weaker ones occur on every continent except for Antarctica. Great Britain, Russia, Australia, and South Africa all experience large numbers of tornadoes. In Japan they are called "dragon whirls."

" The strongest twister I've ever experienced was an F5. **It looked like a giant smoke cloud rising high into the air.** *Branches were flying and trees bending right over until they almost touched the ground—and that was just from the winds on the outside of the tornado.* **I hit the brakes and turned around.** *My foot was shaking on the accelerator. "*

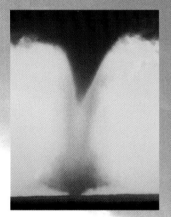

A funnel of whirling air begins to drop downward from the wall cloud.

Low pressure inside the funnel creates a vacuum effect, sucking up dust.

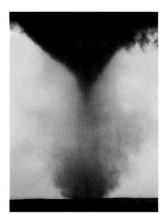

Touchdown! The funnel reaches the ground to become a mature tornado.

Tornado storm cloud

This twister in Texas has descended from the wall cloud, which can be seen flaring out from the base of the storm. The storm cloud may extend to more than twice the height of Mount Everest. Tornadoes form when the rising air in a thunderstorm, called the updraft, begins to rotate.

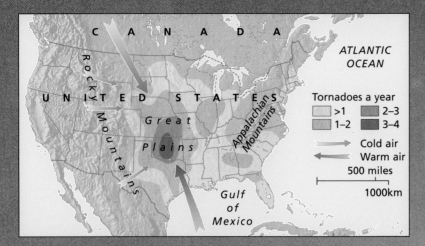

The U.S.'s Great Plains are the world's tornado hot spot. With flat land stretching for many miles and cold winds from Canada and the Rocky Mountains clashing with warm, moist air from the Gulf of Mexico, the conditions in "Tornado Alley" are ideal for twisters.

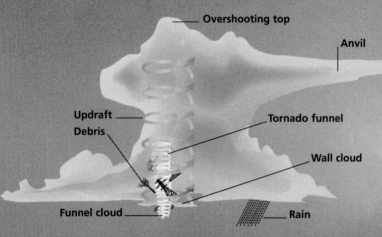

Tornadoes are produced by high-energy thunderstorms, especially a type called a supercell. When the conditions are right, warm air rushes up through the storm so powerfully that the air bursts through the cloud ceiling, forming the overshooting top. This is one of the key signs that a tornado is on its way.

FUJITA SCALE
(wind speed)

FORCE	EFFECT
F0 (40 mph–71 mph)	Damages chimneys. Breaks branches off trees.
F1 (72 mph–111 mph)	Pulls tiles off roofs and overturns mobile homes. Pushes moving vehicles off the road.
F2 (112 mph–156 mph)	Bursts windows. Snaps or uproots large trees.
F3 (157 mph–205 mph)	Tears off roofs and pulls down walls of houses. Can overturn trains and uproot most of a forest.
F4 (206 mph–259 mph)	Flattens buildings. Throws cars through the air.
F5 (260 mph–317 mph)	Rips buildings from the ground. Flings vehicles more than 328 ft. (100m).

The damage caused by a tornado is used to measure its force. This scale was invented by Japanese scientist Tetsuya Theodore Fujita.

PATH OF A TORNADO

In 1925 the Tri-State Tornado cut a terrible trail through Missouri, Illinois, and Indiana, covering around 217 mi. (350km) in four hours. This twister was so big that it did not have a clearly defined funnel. Instead witnesses said it resembled a dark fog rolling toward them. In general, the wider a tornado is, the stronger it is. The Tri-State measured almost one mile across at its base, although it may actually have consisted of two or more funnels, merging in and out of one another. It was the deadliest twister in U.S. history, destroying nine towns and causing almost 700 deaths. However, tornadoes cause the most loss of life in Bangladesh in Asia, where a large number of people live in a small area. In the United States there are many fewer victims now than in the past, mostly because today's networks of storm chasers and meteorologists—scientists who study the weather— can provide earlier warnings.

Twin twisters
These twin tornadoes near Dimmitt, Texas, are weak twisters called land spouts. Supercell storms will often give birth to more than one tornado, but usually the first dies out before the next one forms.

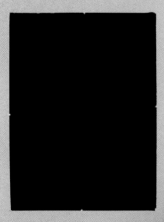

After touchdown the path of a tornado may be a straight line, zigzag, or even a circle.

Destructive winds

This scene of devastation in Happy, Texas, was caused by a tornado in 2002. It also killed two people. The most costly tornado, around Oklahoma City, Oklahoma, in 1999, wrecked more than 2,000 homes and businesses and resulted in $1.2 billion worth of damage. Tornadoes cause the most destruction when they strike built-up areas. On average, Oklahoma City is struck by a damaging twister once every two years.

Flying forks

Tornadoes can snap trees and whip up debris that scrapes bark off trees. This fork was flung into the bare wood of a tree stump by winds of around 186 mph (300km/h) in Saragosa, Texas.

Wide-based tornado

This F3 twister near Laverne, Oklahoma, is around 1,312 ft. (400m) wide. Other tornadoes look more like white pieces of spaghetti. When a tornado has passed its peak intensity, it enters the rope stage. The funnel becomes thinner and leans over to one side. Finally, it dies away.

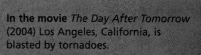

In the movie *The Day After Tomorrow* (2004) Los Angeles, California, is blasted by tornadoes.

TWISTER

Tornadoes can have some unusual effects. Eyewitnesses have reported herds of cattle lifted high up above the ground, wells and rivers sucked dry, and even a train torn from its tracks and set down again—but facing in the opposite direction. What happens inside a tornado is still something of a mystery. However, in 1928, Will Keller, a farmer in Kansas, watched from his storm cellar as a funnel passed overhead. He could see up into a circular opening that rose around 2,460 ft. (750m). Smaller whirlwinds broke away around the edges of the funnel.

THE EFFECTS OF A TORNADO

1 **Subvortex:** A smaller funnel that may twist around the main column

2 **Lightning:** Often occurs with a tornado, sometimes seen flashing inside the funnel

3 **The funnel:** Can be seen owing to the clouds inside and the dust and debris that it has picked up

4 **Crops:** Flattened by the spinning winds, which may make circular patterns similar to crop circles

5 **Wall cloud:** The part of the storm from which the tornado hangs down

6 **Path of destruction:** May crash into one house but leave another almost untouched

7 **Spinning winds:** Reaching 300 mph (500km/h) or more, these are what cause the most damage to homes

8 **Cattle:** Huddle together and often do not move, even when twister is close. Sometimes they are lifted up

9 **Inside the tornado:** Ripped-up plants, dust, and soil, parts of houses, and vehicles are whirled around

10 **A second tornado:** Some storms give birth to more than one twister, but seeing two at once is rare

WAVES AND WATERSPOUTS

When the wind meets the sea, it can create towering waves that are higher than a house. It can also form the twisting columns of clouds and spray known as waterspouts. Most waves are caused by the wind blowing against the surface of the sea. The size of a wave depends on how far it has traveled and the strength of the wind. Storm waves can reach more than 39 ft. (12m) during a gale. The fierce winds of hurricanes, tornadoes, and thunderstorms can sometimes force together groups of waves, creating giant "superwaves." The biggest wave ever recorded was spotted in the Pacific in 1933. From its lowest point, called the trough, to its highest point, or crest, it measured more than 111 ft. (34m)—higher than 14 buses stacked on top of one another.

A famous storm
The movie *The Perfect Storm* (2000) tells the story of the fishing boat *Andrea Gail*, which sank with all of its crew during a huge storm in October 1991. The storm raged along the east coast of North America, from the Caribbean to Canada. Many other crews were saved by the coast guard and navy helicopters.

The power of storm waves
Spray from an enormous wave washes over the 98-ft. (30-m)-high Le Four lighthouse in Brittany, France. Storm waves can even pose a threat to oil rigs and can tip over large ships or smash them into pieces.

Storm surges

In 1965 Hurricane Betsy sent surf crashing into hotels lining Miami Beach, Florida. As well as whipping up enormous waves, hurricanes cause the sea level beneath them to rise. The seawater sweeps over the coast and through towns and farms. The deadliest storm surges are in Bangladesh.

Water whirlwinds

Waterspouts are columns of whirling air that occur over seas and lakes. They are usually narrower than tornadoes and reach up to around 1,640 ft. (500m)—as high as the world's tallest building. Waterspouts may look like they are made out of spray, but the funnel actually contains water vapor from the air. Sometimes they suck up sea creatures such as fish, clams, and jellyfish, which then fall inland as very strange rain.

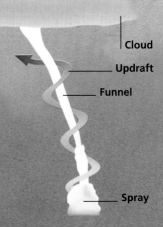

Cloud

Updraft

Funnel

Spray

Some waterspouts are tornadoes over water, but most do not need severe storms in order to form. Air above a warm sea, such as in tropical areas, rises rapidly, creating an updraft. Rotating air currents close to the sea surface cause the updraft to spin. The low pressure inside the funnel sucks up spray at the bottom, while the top links to a cloud.

" A bright flash of **lightning lit up a huge wall of water** *less than 100 feet away from where I was standing.* **I had come face-to-face with a storm surge.** *In the morning I saw the results—piles of dead fish, clothing, and a ruined boat.* **Even the palm trees had been turned into battered stumps** *by the force of the water. "*

Multiple waterspouts

This line of waterspouts was seen off the coast of Albania. Waterspouts last for around 15 minutes and are usually too weak to cause much damage. However, in 1969 a swarm of six came ashore in Cyprus in just a few hours and killed four people.

DUST STORMS

In deserts and other dry areas winds may whip up storms of sand and dust that are so vast that they can be seen from space. Sometimes the hot conditions also produce whirlwinds of superheated air called dust devils. As a dust storm approaches, birds sound warning cries, and certain animals, such as camels, bellow with alarm. In the distance the storm looks like a solid bank of clouds rising from the ground. It arrives as a wave of tumbling, choking dust. The dust cloud can be 4,920 ft. (1,500m) tall, almost four times the height of the Empire State Building in New York City. The grains of dust may drift for thousands of miles, high up in the atmosphere. Sand from the Sahara desert in Africa falls as far away as northern Europe and the Amazon in South America.

" The winds around a dust devil are strong enough to knock you over, but once you are inside, it is strangely still. It is as hot as an oven in there, and as the Sun filters through the spinning wall of desert grit, it creates this weird orange glow. Up above, tumbleweeds and dust dance around, but beyond them, the funnel opens up into blue sky. "

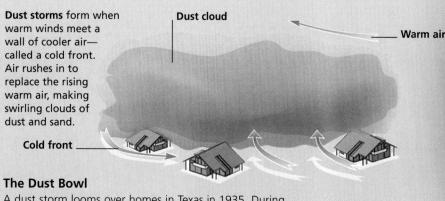

Dust storms form when warm winds meet a wall of cooler air—called a cold front. Air rushes in to replace the rising warm air, making swirling clouds of dust and sand.

Dust cloud

Warm air

Cold front

The Dust Bowl
A dust storm looms over homes in Texas in 1935. During the 1930s dust storms devastated an area from Kansas to New Mexico, which became known as the "Dust Bowl." Many farmers and their families had to leave because the soil was blown away, destroying their farmland.

Braving the sand
Children battle a dust storm in Xiahe, China. Sand blows across the country from the Taklimakan desert in the northeast and the Gobi desert to the north. Dust storms are common in deserts, but they also form in other regions where the soil has become dry and dusty. This can happen when there is a long drought and where there are few plants to hold the soil together.

Desert whirlwinds

Dust devils, like this one in Tucson, Arizona, are spinning funnels of air that are visible because of the dust, twigs, and other debris that they pick up. These small whirlwinds do not usually cause much damage, but some are powerful enough to overturn a car. Dust devils are formed in deserts and other places where the ground is hot and the conditions are dry. They can range in height from just a few feet to around a mile high.

Red sky in the city

A dust cloud engulfs Beijing, China, turning day into night. Drivers cannot see well, so traffic moves slowly, and airports have to be closed. As the dust passes over cities and factories, it picks up pollution, which will spread to wherever the dust takes it.

Wind

Dust and debris

Funnel

Heated ground

Dust devils form when the Sun beats down on open land, strongly heating the air above the ground so that it rises as an updraft. A section of air may then begin to rotate because it is whipped around by winds blowing in the area.

SOLAR WINDS

It is not only Earth that has wild weather. On the Sun, storms produced by sunspots—the dark patches on its surface—throw bursts of particles out into space. These form part of the solar wind that "blows" from the Sun throughout our galaxy. One million tons of particles per second stream out and produce auroras hundreds of miles above the surface of Earth. These stunning light displays appear in different forms, including bands of light, bright arches, and rippling curtains of reds, blues, and greens. You usually need to be close to the Arctic or Antarctic circles in order to see them. The Inuit people of Labrador, in northeast Canada, believe that these displays are torches carried by spirits to show them the way to heaven.

Aurora Australis
The green glow of the *Aurora Australis* over Antarctica was photographed from the space shuttle. When the Sun's storms are at their peak, which happens every 11 years, the *Aurora Borealis* may be seen on Earth as far south as Athens, Greece, and the *Aurora Australis* as far north as Brisbane, Australia.

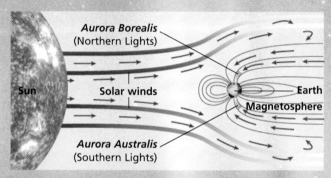

Earth is surrounded by an invisible envelope of magnetic force—called the magnetosphere. The part of the magnetosphere facing the Sun is rounded, while the other side forms a tail like that of a comet. Particles from the solar wind find their way into the magnetosphere through the tail and are carried toward the poles. When they crash into gases in Earth's atmosphere, light is released, creating the auroras.

Aurora Borealis
Also known as the Northern Lights, here the *Aurora Borealis* illuminates the sky in Finland. In the Southern Hemisphere this effect is called the *Aurora Australis*, or Southern Lights.

FIRE AND ICE

EXTREME HEAT

The highest temperature ever recorded was near the coast of Libya in north Africa. In September 1922 it reached a searing 136°F (57.8°C). Deserts, which occur where the annual rainfall is less than 9.75 in. (25cm), experience some of the most extreme heat on the planet. The most dramatic changes of temperature within one day also happen there. During daylight hours the clear skies mean that the Sun constantly beats down. After dark there is no protective blanket of clouds to hold onto the warmth, so the temperature can suddenly drop, sometimes to freezing. But hot, dry weather is found from the Mediterranean region to Australia. And during a heat wave even countries with normally mild climates are exposed to days or weeks of scorching sunshine.

Rain-forest humidity
In the rain forests that are found toward the equator, such as this one in Costa Rica, it is both hot and wet. The temperature rarely goes above 93°F (34°C), but the humidity level—the amount of water vapor in the air—is high. These areas may receive 260 in. (6,500mm) of rain per year, ten times as much as in London, England.

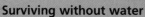

Drought in the Sahel
At this refugee camp in Darfur, Sudan, people are lining up at the only well. Millions of people had to leave their villages because of war, but extreme weather also played a part. Darfur is in the Sahel, a dry area south of the Sahara that is kept from becoming a desert only by the seasonal rains. There were poor rains for many years, making it difficult for any crops to grow.

Surviving without water
Catfish are able to survive even when rivers and lakes have dried up into puddles. Some catfish can breathe through their skin instead of their gills and bury themselves in the mud. Others wiggle across land for short distances to find a pool containing more water.

Imaginary lake
This pool in the Australian outback is a mirage—an optical illusion usually seen over deserts or other flat, treeless areas. When the air close to the ground gets very hot, it bends light so that objects above the horizon appear to be below it. Because the sky is blue, the mirage looks like the shimmering water of a lake.

Relief from the heat
A spray of water created by a broken pipe keeps these children cool during a heat wave. Periods of unusually high temperatures can be deadly. In 2003 a heat wave across Europe killed 27,000 people.

A water source
Villagers flock to this well in Gujarat, India, because the reservoirs, wells, and ponds in neighboring areas have dried up. During a drought people may have to travel long distances to find water or must wait hours for tankers to arrive with supplies of freshwater from other parts of the country.

DROUGHT RELIEF

The effects of a drought are most devastating in regions that are already hot and dry. Around one billion people throughout the world live in this type of environment, where water is in short supply and the soil is only just good enough to farm. If the rainfall is lower than usual, it tips the balance. As crops fail and animals become sick, a famine can follow. Many people may starve as a result unless they receive help. Eventually, the weather pattern changes. Even the 30-year drought in the Sahel area of Africa came to an end in the 1980s. Today scientists are finding ways to predict changes in rainfall patterns, which are linked to the movement of ocean currents such as El Niño. In the future they may be able to forecast when and where droughts are likely to happen so that people have more time to prepare.

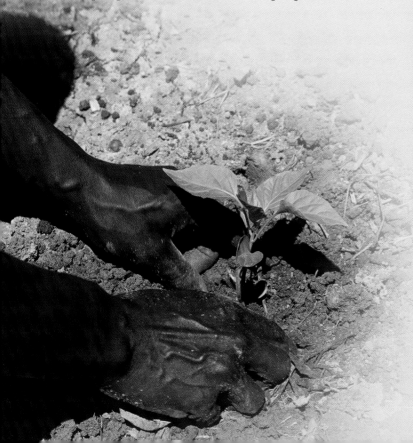

Watering hole
This herd of African buffalo is drinking from a pool refilled by rain. A drought can destroy the habitats where wild birds, fish, and animals live. As a result, endangered species are more likely to become extinct, but many creatures survive by migrating to less affected areas.

Desert bloom
These flowers in the Mojave Desert, in California, bloom after the winter rains. They complete their entire life cycle—from shoot to flower to seed—in the few weeks before the summer heat begins. The hardy seeds then wait until the next rain shower.

Replanting the forests
Since 1977 the Green Belt Movement has been involved in planting 30 million trees in Kenya and other African countries. Deforestation, when trees are cut down for farming or timber, makes soil more likely to turn into dust. The new trees will help reduce the effects of droughts.

DROUGHTS

It begins when the expected rains fail. Plants start to wilt and then shrivel up. Trees drop their leaves to stop them from losing water. The soil is baked as hard as concrete or turns to dust that is blown away by the wind. In extremely dry forests wildfires may blaze out of control. Reservoirs empty and rivers become a trickle or disappear, while livestock, such as cattle and sheep, struggle to find enough to eat. A severe drought can have a devastating impact on local wildlife, farming, and people, and its effects can last for many years. A drought happens when less rain than normal falls over a period of several weeks or longer. This can occur anywhere, including Sudan, the United States, Australia, and even the Amazon rain forest.

Animals become sick
A prolonged drought has weakened these cattle, belonging to the Samburu herders of Kenya. Grazing areas and water are hard to find, so animals are more likely to become sick or to die from hunger.

37

The ground dries up

The Atacama Desert in Chile is the driest place on our planet. Showers occur only a few times every 100 years, and the average yearly rainfall is less than an inch. When there is no rain, reservoirs and riverbeds like this one dry up.

Crops die out

The plants that are naturally found in drier regions have adapted so that they can live with little rain or can regrow quickly after a drought. But crops such as this corn plant need enough water in order to produce the fruits and seeds that we eat. In a drought the harvest will be smaller, or crops may die completely.

Breaking the drought

The arrival of rain brings welcome relief for these villagers in Somalia. Some droughts end slowly, as rainfall gradually returns to normal. Others are broken with a sudden torrential downpour. Where the soil is baked hard, this can bring its own problems—such as flooding.

A relief camp

Famine drives large numbers of people away from their homelands as they seek out desperately needed food, water, and medicine. Many people, like these children, find shelter and a meal in relief camps.

International aid

The Red Cross, the United Nations (UN), and governments and charities worldwide send emergency food relief to areas where there is a famine. After the drought has ended, people begin to rebuild their lives, digging wells to provide water and planting new crops.

WILDFIRES

Every year tens of thousands of wildfires begin around the world. Some are small and burn themselves out, while others billow into huge walls of flames that blacken hillsides and turn buildings into scorched ruins. In the United States a total area of 6,630 square miles—almost as large as Israel—burns in an average year. These fires are most common in California, Australia, and the south of France, where the types of plants and weather conditions make it easy for wildfires to develop. Sweet-smelling trees and bushes, such as eucalyptus, are filled with oils that act like fire lighters, while the hot Sun and droughts dry out plants and timber. Warm winds then fan the flames and drive the fires onward at speeds up to 15.5 mph (25km/h).

City in danger
A fire in the Catalina hills around Tucson, Arizona, heads toward the city. Around one half of all wildfires are sparked by lightning. Many others are started deliberately or caused by human carelessness, including by cigarettes and campfires that have not been put out properly.

Fiery weather
Clouds called pyrocumulus sometimes form as the hot air from a wildfire rises, taking moisture along with it. These clouds may also bring lightning, which can start more fires. The smoke from wildfires drifts high up into the atmosphere, turning sunsets deep orange and red.

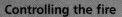

Controlling the fire

This airplane is spraying a fire retardant—a mixture of chemicals that will cool and slow the flames. Firefighting teams on the ground and in the air work together very closely. Weather updates are crucial when tackling wildfires because the wind affects the fire's speed and direction.

Quick-spreading fires

Some fires burn along the ground, but others, called crown fires, leap from the top of one tree to the next. Gusts of wind may send hot embers into the air and then start new blazes. Ferocious fires can even create spinning funnels of wind, called fire whirls, that hurl burning logs through the air.

OUT OF THE FLAMES

Wildfires are destructive and deadly, but they are also a natural process. Some trees release their seeds only after being burned or need fires to clear away other plants so that their seedlings can reach the light. In the forests of California fires are a vital part of the giant redwood tree's life cycle. Wildfires clear decayed logs and diseased plants, while ashes make soil more fertile. The result is that new growth can flourish in the place of old.

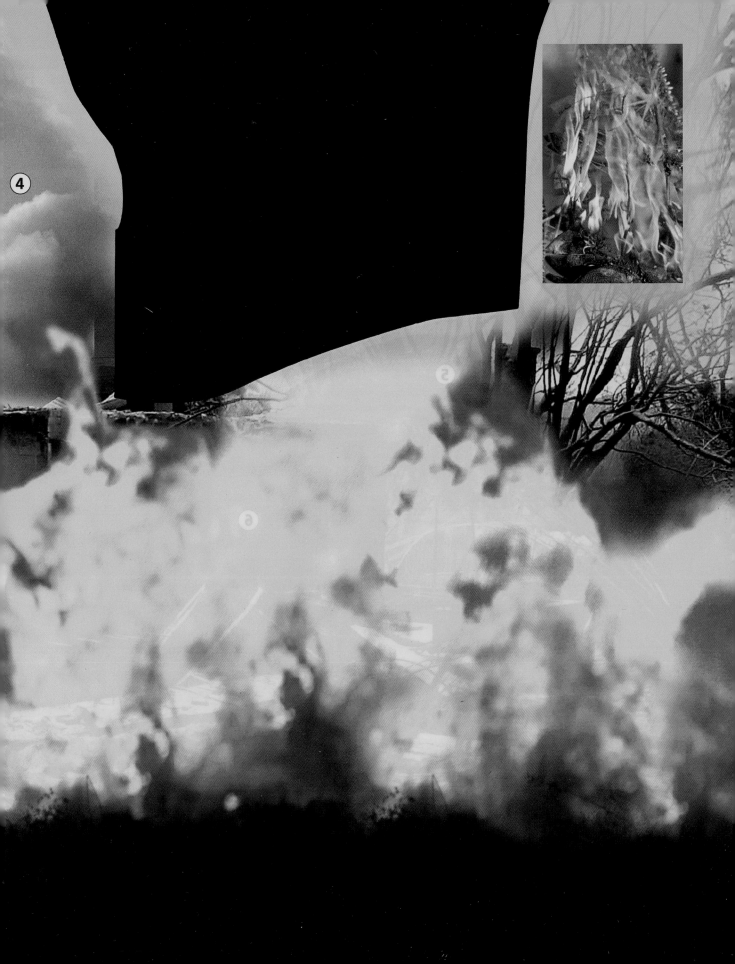

WHAT HAPPENS IN A WILDFIRE

1 Firefighting helicopter: Carries a container that can drop hundreds of gallons of water onto the flames below

2 Far hillside: Even trees many miles away are not safe if the wind blows in this direction

3 Firefighters: May use hoses on smaller fires and build firebreaks to stop blazes from spreading

4 Smoke: Will stream out as it is blown by the wind, showing where the fire will move next

5 Bare hill: With no protective plants, heavy rains can lead to flooding and mud slides

6 Burned-out building: Many homes are so badly damaged that they cannot be repaired. Often people move away

7 Blooming again: Some plants, such as this catspaw, flower better after a fire

8 Charred tree: Thick bark can give protection from the flames

Fireproof seeds

This seed pod, from an Australian bush called banksia, looks like it has been burned up. But it can survive a fire even if the plant itself has been killed. In fact, the heat makes the seed cases open up, and new banksias will grow as soon as it rains.

SNOW

A deep, muffled "thunk" is the sound that marks the beginning of the deadliest type of avalanche. It is the noise of hundreds of thousands of tons of snow cracking away from a mountainside and shattering like a huge pane of glass. In a blizzard snowflakes are whipped into an icy storm, but avalanches are snowy weather at its most extreme. As the snow sheet roars downhill, it gathers up deadly ice chunks and rocks along the way. It can also generate high-speed winds that can snap trees and rip roofs from houses. When the avalanche stops, the debris sets like cement in a few seconds, making it impossible to dig your way out without help. Those who have survived the impact of an avalanche are very lucky—only one in 20 victims is rescued alive.

Crystal stars
Snowflakes grow into different shapes depending on the weather conditions high up in the clouds where they form.

Snowstorm
Snowplows cleared the streets of New York City after it was brought to a standstill by one of the worst blizzards in the city's history, in 2003. Blizzards occur when strong winds and heavy snow combine.

Life in the Antarctic
These emperor penguins can survive colder temperatures than any other animal. A layer of fat and thick, downy feathers protect them from icy winds that blow at up to 124 mph (200km/h).

How avalanches form

Loose powder avalanches, such as this one in Antarctica, occur when light snow cascades off a mountain. They usually start from a single point and get wider as they fall farther. Slab avalanches are much more dangerous. A huge plate of snow breaks free and thunders down at speeds of 60 mph (100km/h) or more. If a slope is good for skiing, it is at risk of an avalanche.

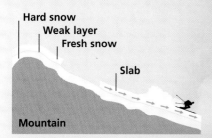

Hard snow
Weak layer
Fresh snow
Slab
Mountain

A slab avalanche forms when a heavy fall of new snow—or existing snow blown by the wind—piles up quickly on top of a weak layer. The weight becomes too heavy, and the weak layer of snow cracks, sending the slab sliding down. In many cases a skier or a snowmobiler is the trigger.

Avalanche rescue

These rescuers are using long poles, called probes, to find exactly where a victim is buried. Sniffer dogs and the radio signals from devices called beacons can also help locate people.

Destruction in Galtür

It took only 50 seconds for a huge wall of snow and rubble, 328 ft. (100m) high and weighing 300,000 tons, to smash through this Austrian village in 1999, killing 31 people.

Ice storm
A strong, cold wind has driven drops of freezing rain onto one side of this tree in Switzerland. During the ice storm they blew along the surface and then froze solid.

ICE

Most of Earth's water is locked up as ice. In the winter the ice sheets that cover the land and oceans at the North and South poles spread over more than 11 million square miles in total—an area so big that it would cover all of Africa. Extreme cold can be fatal for humans, but icy weather is destructive in other ways too. Icebergs can sink ships—the most famous, the *Titanic*, was lost in the North Atlantic with 1,517 passengers and crew in 1912. In an ice storm pouring rain freezes to form a glaze of ice that can be almost 8 in. (20cm) thick. Roads become dangerously slippery, and power supplies fail as cables break under the weight. Hail can also be deadly. In 1986 hailstones, many weighing more than two pounds, killed 92 people in Bangladesh.

Iceberg islands
These icebergs close to Antarctica are breaking off an ice shelf, a thick sheet of ice covering the sea. Nine tenths of an iceberg lies underwater, which is why they are a danger to ships. The largest iceberg ever recorded was half the size of Wales.

Balls of ice
Hailstones form in thunderclouds. A tiny ice crystal is coated with layer upon layer of ice as it is blown around inside a cloud. When the hailstone becomes too heavy for the updraft—the wind that blows upward—to keep it in the air, it falls to the ground. The largest hailstones ever reported were said to be the size of pumpkins.

Building with ice
Every year the Icehotel in Kiruna, Lapland, is rebuilt using 3,000 tons of ice and large amounts of snow. The idea was inspired by the igloos of the Inuit people, made from snow carved into blocks.

*" Hail can be from pea-sized to grapefruit-sized or more. I've had **hail the size of tennis balls hit the truck** and leave large dents. It is probably **the scariest thing a storm chaser runs into.** Imagine driving down the street and people throwing fist-sized rocks. "*

Frozen waterfalls
When a waterfall freezes, it provides a challenging vertical sheet of ice for climbers. During winters with a long cold spell even Niagara Falls on the U.S.-Canadian border will freeze over. At more than half a mile wide, it is the world's second-largest falls. The river does not stop flowing, but the falling water can make ice mounds that are almost 50 ft. (15m) thick. A bridge of ice may also link the two banks.

GLOSSARY

Air pressure The pressure exerted by the atmosphere, measured as the weight of air pressing on a given area.

Anvil The flat top of a thundercloud, which resembles the heavy steel block used by blacksmiths.

Atmosphere The blanket of gases that extends almost 500 mi. (800km) above Earth.

Auroras The Northern Lights and Southern Lights, caused by the solar wind.

Avalanche A mass of loose snow or a huge snow slab moving rapidly down a slope.

Beaufort scale A scale from 0 to 12 that classifies the strength of a wind by its effects on the landscape.

Blizzard A combination of heavy snow and high winds producing severe weather.

Broadscale flooding Floods across a wide area, when heavy rain over a long period saturates the soil and makes rivers overflow.

Cirrus Strands of clouds that form above 16,400 ft. (5,000m) and are blown into streaks.

Climate The general weather conditions in a region over a long period.

Cold front The front edge of a mass of cold air.

Cumulonimbus A cumulus cloud that produces heavy rain, hail, and thunderstorms.

Cumulus A tall, puffy cloud that forms when "packages" of warmed air rise and cool.

Cyclone 1. The name for a hurricane in the south Pacific or Indian oceans; 2. A rotating low pressure system.

Desert An area with almost no vegetation and little rain.

Drought When less rain than normal falls in a region for an extended time.

Dust Bowl The Great Plains and Midwest of the U.S. in the 1930s, when heat waves, droughts, and overfarming caused dust storms.

Dust devil A column of spinning air and dust.

Dust storm A vast moving cloud of dust that reduces visibility to less than one mile.

El Niño A warm current in the Pacific Ocean that affects global weather patterns.

Electric charge A property of all particles. When large charges build up in clouds, they can cause lightning.

Equator The imaginary line around the middle of Earth that divides the Northern Hemisphere from the Southern Hemisphere.

Evaporation When liquid water turns into water vapor.

Eye The calm, often cloudless center of a hurricane.

Eye wall The ring of storm clouds around the eye.

Flash flood A sudden flood, usually as a result of intense rain in a small area.

Fujita scale A scale from F0 to F5 that rates the strength of tornadoes based on the damage they have caused.

Funnel A cone or column of spinning air, as in a tornado or a dust devil.

Funnel cloud The cloud inside a tornado funnel, formed because low pressure makes the water vapor in the air become droplets.

Gale A strong wind blowing at around 30 mph (50km/h).

High pressure When air is sinking down in an area. It often brings clear skies.

Hurricane An intense storm born in the tropics with winds of 74 mph (119km/h) or more.

Ice storm A storm of freezing cold rain that sets to a solid glaze of ice when it hits the ground or objects.

Landfall When a hurricane crosses from sea onto land.

Low pressure When air is rising up in an area.

Magnetosphere The region of space, like an invisible envelope around the planet, where Earth's magnetic field has an effect.

Mammatus Clumps of clouds that hang from the anvil of a thundercloud.

Meteorologist A person who studies the science of weather.

Mirage An optical illusion often seen in deserts, usually taking the form of a pool of shimmering water.

Mud slide When water-soaked soil turns to mud and slides down a slope.

Ocean current A movement of water, like a river in an ocean, often caused by winds.

Overshooting top A dome rising above the anvil of a thundercloud, caused by extremely strong updrafts.

Pyrocumulus A cumulus cloud that is formed when moist air is forced to rise by the heat of a wildfire.

Saffir-Simpson scale A scale from Category 1 to Category 5 used to rate the strength of hurricanes.

Solar wind A stream of particles from the Sun.

Storm chaser Someone who tracks and travels in search of severe storms.

Storm surge The rise in sea level caused by an area of low pressure and its winds. Hurricanes create the most extreme storm surges.

Stratus The lowest type of cloud, formed when a large amount of warm, moist air rises gently.

Subvortex A smaller funnel inside or around the main funnel of a tornado. Plural: Subvortices.

Thundercloud A powerful cumulonimbus cloud that produces lightning.

Tornado A violently rotating column of wind, which extends from a storm cloud and touches the ground.

Tropical storm A storm that begins in the tropics. A very strong tropical storm is called a hurricane, cyclone, or typhoon, depending on its location.

Tropics The region north and south of the equator between the Tropic of Cancer and the Tropic of Capricorn.

Tsunami An enormous wave caused by an earthquake on the ocean floor.

Typhoon The name for a hurricane in the northwest Pacific Ocean.

Updraft An air current that moves vertically upward.

Wall cloud A portion of a cloud at the bottom of a storm, from which tornadoes may descend.

Water cycle The constant movement of water between the oceans, air, and land.

Water vapor Water in its gas form.

Waterspout A funnel of spinning wind over water.

Wildfire An uncontrolled fire in forests, the bush, or grassland. Known in Australia as a bushfire.

INDEX

Publisher: Sue Grabham
Editor: Clive Wilson
Additional editorial: Simon Holland,
  Stephanie Pliakas
Senior designer: Carol Ann Davis
Additional design:
  Heidi Appleton, Mike Davis,
  and Malcolm Parchment
Picture research manager:
  Cee Weston-Baker
DTP manager: Nicky Studdart
Production manager:
  Nancy Roberts
Indexer and proofreader:
  Sheila Clewley
Consultant: Wayne Elliott,
  Met Office, U.K.
Additional research: Carol Ann Davis

KINGFISHER

a Houghton Mifflin Company
  imprint
222 Berkeley Street
Boston, Massachusetts 02116
www.houghtonmifflinbooks.com

First published in 2005
10 9 8 7 6 5 4 3 2 1
1TR/0705/TWP/CLSN(CLSN)/150ENSO/F

LIBRARY OF CONGRESS CATALOGING-IN-
PUBLICATION DATA
Harris, Caroline, 1964–
Kingfisher voyages: wild weather/
Caroline Harris—1st ed.
  p. cm.
Includes index.
ISBN-13: 978-0-7534-5911-9
ISBN-10: 0-7534-5911-6
1. Weather—Juvenile literature. 2.
Storms—Juvenile literature. I. Title:
Wild weather. II. Title.
QC981.3.H367 2005
551.55—dc22
2005010925

Printed in Singapore

ACKNOWLEDGMENTS

The publisher would like to thank the following for permission to reproduce their material. Every care has been taken to trace copyright holders. However, if there have been unintentional omissions or failure to trace copyright holders, we apologize and will, if informed, endeavor to make corrections in any future edition.

Key: *b* = bottom, *c* = center, *l* = left, *r* = right, *t* = top

Cover Warren Faidley/Photolibrary.com; back cover *l* Corbis/William James Warren; back cover *r* Science Photo Library/Kenneth Libbrecht (SPL); pages 1 Corbis Kevin R. Morris; 2*tl* Warren Faidley; 2*cl* Associated Press; 2–3*b* Photolibrary.com/ Warren Faidley; 3*tl* Warren Faidley; 3*r* Warren Faidley; 4 SPL/Susan McCartney; 4*b* Corbis/Sergio Pitamitz; 5*c* Getty Photographer's Choice; 5*b* Getty Photographer's Choice; 6 Corbis/Reuters; 7 Alamy/Steve Bloom; 8–9 Getty Stone; 8*bl* Rex Features; 9*tl* Photolibrary.com; 9*tr* Warren Faidley; 9*tcr* Warren Faidley; 9*cr* Corbis/Paul Souders; 9*cr* SPL/Pascal Goetgheluck; 9*br* Warren Faidley; 9*br* Alamy; 10*l* National Oceanic and Atmospheric Administration, U.S.; 10*br* Getty; 11*bl* Warren Faidley; 11*tr* SPL/Peter Menzel; 11*bl* Corbis/Jim Reed; 12–13 Corbis/Tim Davis; Warren Faidley; Photolibrary.com; Getty Stone; 14*tr* Rex Features; 14 Associated Press; 14–15*b* Rex Features; 16*t* Warren Faidley; 16*c* Corbis/Sygma; 16*b* Photolibrary.com; 17 Getty Imagebank; 18*cl* National Oceanic and Atmospheric Administration, U.S.; 19*tl* Corbis/Reuters; 19*tc* Corbis/Sygma; 18–19*c* Corbis/Bettmann; 20*tr* Getty Stone; 20 Warren Faidley; 21*t* Photolibrary.com; 21*b* Corbis/Roger Ball; 22–23 Warren Faidley; 24 Warren Faidley; 25*tr* Warren Faidley; 25*c* Warren Faidley; 25*cr* Warren Faidley; 25*br* Kobal; 26–27 Getty Imagebank; Getty Taxi; Corbis/Peter Beck; Corbis/Kevin R. Morris; Warren Faidley; 28*l* Corbis/Jean Gulchard; 28*cr* Corbis/Sygma; 29*tl* Rex Features; 29*bl* Frank Lane Picture Agency; 30*bl* National Oceanic and Atmospheric Administration, U.S.; Corbis/Michael Yamashita; 31*t* Corbis/Lio Lingun; 31*r* Warren Faidley; 32 SPL/Pekka Parviainen; 32*tr* Corbis; 34–35 Still Pictures; 34*tl* Photolibrary.com; 34*bl* Photolibrary.com; 35*t* Photolibrary.com; 35*br* Corbis/Bettmann; 36*l* Corbis/Adrian Arbib; 37*bl* Corbis/Wendy Stone; 37*tr* Corbis/Peter Johnson; 37*cr* Corbis; 38–39 Corbis/Reuters; 40 Corbis/David Turnley; 40 Corbis/Viviane Moos; 40*b* Corbis/Chris Rainier; 41 Photolibrary.com; 41*br* Corbis/Richard Hamilton Smith; 42–43 Getty Stone; 42*tr* Alamy/A. T. Willett; 42*cl* Corbis; 43*tr* Corbis/ Vince Streano; 44–45 Photolibrary.com; Getty News; ANT Photolibrary, Australia; Still Pictures; 46*tr* SPL; 46*cr* Alamy/Richard Levine; 46*b* Frank Lane Picture Agency; 47*t* Still Pictures; 47*bl* Corbis/Reuters; 47*br* Corbis/Sygma; 48*tl* Rex Features; 48*cl* SPL/Jim Reed; 48*b* Frank Lane Picture Agency; 49*tl* Getty Robert Harding Picture Library; 49*r* Photolibrary.com; 50–51 Photolibrary.com; 52–53 Corbis/Paul Souder; 54 Photolibrary.com

The publisher would like to thank the following illustrators:
4–5 Jurgen Ziewe (Lightning strikes); 26–27 Peter Bull (Twister); 44–45 Mike Davis (Out of the flames); 4–5, 6, 18–19, 23, 29, 30–31, 32 Peter Winfield (weather artwork)